# Memories of

# SEONG MIN YOO

MEMORIES OF KOREA
SEONG MIN YOO

Tumbleweed Books
*Tumble through the pages of our books*

Memories of Korea / Seong min Yoo

ISBN 978-1-928094-20-3
EISBN 978-1-928074-23-4

The artwork in this book was rendered in watercolor, the text Kristine ITC and Minion Pro.
Edit and layout by Douglas Owen
Artwork and story by Seong min Yoo

10 9 8 7 6 5 4 3 2 1

This is a story of one little girl's adventures in a far off country and the valuable experiences she gained while there.

The book tells about the importance of family bonds, no matter where they are living.

For my loving parents, and Valerie and Scott

This was my first time visiting Korea, Mommy's home country, since I was born in Canada. I looked forward to meeting my cousin Minhee for the first time. I saw her in a picture, and she was a little girl, just like me.

Mommy and I arrived at the airport after almost 12 hours flying. It was a long flight, but I slept most of the time, except for the 3 hours before the plane landed.

The airport was quiet and there weren't many people around, but I was very excited, when I suddenly heard a voice from far away call out loudly, "Valerie!" I looked around quickly to see Halmoni (Grandma) standing in front of me, smiling and patting my face. Halmoni said softly, "It was a really long trip, wasn't it?"

I saw a little girl with wide eyes, holding something tight with her little hands. It was my cousin, and she handed what she held to me and blushed without saying a word. It was a soft stuffed toy and it felt just like Mommy's hands.

After one week of rest, Minhee came over to visit me at Halmoni's house. She was shy at first, but as we got more comfortable, we read books, played the piano and had so much fun.

Around noon, we set the table together for lunch and she even showed me how to use chopsticks, which I had never used before.

Later that afternoon, we went to the market. There were so many interesting people and sights to see. There were voices everywhere of sellers and buyers negotiating prices. There were different kinds of street food on the little cart with four wheels on it, like chicken skewers, spicy hot rice cakes and twisted sugary donuts, just to name a few.

Then Mommy and Halmoni took me to a cutlery store and bought chopsticks with three holes for my fingers, so that I could practice. They are still not easy to use, but I always enjoy using them, especially for eating noodles.

A few days later we went to Seoul Grand Park with our family. A giant animal statue stood in front of the entrance. We posed for a few seconds so Mommy could take pictures of us and we saw many beautiful cherry blossom trees everywhere.

On the way we found a little pagoda where there was a square floor made of oak, with four beams in the corners. We took a rest in this nice cool place and looked at the clear blue sky. We were tired, but had a very good time.

When we got home, Halmoni gave me a nice bath. As the water splashed all over me, I felt sure that it was one of the best baths ever.

The next day, Mommy said we didn't have many days left until we had to leave. The last place we visited was Mommy's grandparent's grave in the southern province near Seoul.

Mommy prepared some food and brought two bunches of beautiful white flowers.

The first thing Halabugi (Grandpa) did was set the table. Halabugi said it was made out of stone and he put the food that we had brought on it. He said the smell of food will make the ancestors happy. We all bowed to their graves and were still for a minute. I saw Mommy's eyes glisten. Maybe the picture of their memories got into her eyes. At that time, a cool breeze blew over us and it felt much nicer.

Finally, it was our last day before we had to return home. I saw Halmoni go inside her bedroom, and she soon came out holding a box. She handed it to me to open.

Inside, I saw a beautiful red dress. She lovingly took it out and put it on me. It felt really good. "It's called a Hanbok," she said. "It's a traditional Korean costume." It had a red skirt and multi-coloured stripes on its arms, and there were two long ribbons on the chest that could be tied to make a bow. "It's yours! I hope you like it." Halmoni touched my hair gently saying, "I can't wait to see you grown up and see you again."

"Don't forget that you are part Korean, and you should always be proud of it and blessed that you can learn the cultures of two countries."

Now every time I wear the Hanbok, it reminds me of those wonderful times I spent in Korea. How happy I was being with family. I have realized that when the time with family is short, it becomes more precious every day.

CPSIA information can be obtained at www.ICGtesting.com
Printed in the USA
LVIW01n2009250717
542598LV00010B/212